M'm! M'm!
HOMEMADE
IN MINUTES

You Can Take It Easy...

Because *Campbell's* Makes It Easy To Create Delicious Homemade Meals In Just Minutes

Your days are hectic. Never-ending rounds of running here, hurrying there. And no matter where the scurrying takes you, it inevitably reaches the "What's for Dinner?" dilemma.

Trust **Campbell's** to solve it deliciously with this collection of over 75 exciting and new home-cooked meals, quick and easy to make in just 30 minutes or less!

Serve Chicken Quesadillas (20 minutes), Chicken & Broccoli Alfredo (25 minutes), Beef & Broccoli (30 minutes), Asian Chicken Stir-Fry (25 minutes), Fiesta Taco Salad (25 minutes), Easy Chicken & Pasta (30 minutes) and many more simple and "souprising" meals your family will love.

- Meals that are quick and contemporary, taste-tempting and timesaving.

- Ready from start to serve in 30 minutes or less.

- Made with the care of your home cooking and the convenience of **Campbell's.**

Now dinner is no longer a dilemma... it's a delight!

Timesaving Tips

To have cooked rice and pasta readily available when called for in a recipe, take advantage of these make-ahead tips.

Rice

Prepare rice ahead and freeze in 1-cup containers. To serve, place 2 frozen 1-cup portions in a microwave-safe bowl. Add 2 tablespoons of chicken broth or water and cover with waxed paper. Microwave on HIGH 5 minutes or until heated through, stirring once.

Pasta

Pre-cook and drain pasta following package directions. Toss with a little oil to prevent sticking, and refrigerate small portions for 3 to 5 days in shallow sealed containers. For longer storage, place the sealed containers in the freezer. Defrost pasta in the refrigerator. To reheat, place in a colander and immerse in hot water just long enough to heat through,1 to 3 minutes. Or, place thawed pasta in a microwave-safe bowl. Cover and microwave on HIGH 2 to 4 minutes or until hot, stirring once.

More!

• For pre-cooked chicken, substitute a 5-ounce can of SWANSON Premium Chunk Chicken Breast or Chunk Chicken for ¾ to 1 cup cooked chicken.

• Pre-cut fresh vegetables from the salad bar or produce aisle will cut preparation time. Pre-sliced beef and chicken are also available in most supermarkets.

• Save time by overlapping steps. While water is boiling or chicken is browning, chop vegetables, measure seasonings and open cans.

• To quick-thaw frozen vegetables, remove from the packaging and place in a microwave-safe bowl. Cover with waxed paper and microwave on HIGH 2 or 3 minutes, breaking apart with a fork every 30 seconds until easily separated but not cooked. Or, follow directions to microwave on packaging.

• Warm up tortillas for easier handling. Stack tortillas and wrap in damp paper towels. Microwave on HIGH for 15 seconds for 2 tortillas; add 15 seconds to time for every 2 additional tortillas.

POULTRY IN NO TIME

Chicken & Broccoli Alfredo

Prep Time: 10 minutes   **Cook Time:** 15 minutes

6 ounces *uncooked* fettuccine
1 cup fresh *or* frozen broccoli flowerets
2 tablespoons butter *or* margarine
1 pound skinless, boneless chicken breasts, cubed
1 can (10¾ ounces) CAMPBELL'S Condensed Cream of Mushroom Soup *or* 98% Fat Free Cream of Mushroom Soup
½ cup milk
⅓ cup grated Parmesan cheese
¼ teaspoon freshly ground pepper

1. Prepare fettuccine according to package directions. Add broccoli for last 4 minutes of cooking time. Drain.

2. In medium skillet over medium-high heat, heat butter. Add chicken and cook until browned, stirring often.

3. Add soup, milk, cheese, pepper and fettuccine mixture and cook through, stirring often.   *Serves 4*

Chicken & Broccoli Alfredo

Asian Chicken Stir-Fry

(photo on front cover)

Prep Time: 5 minutes   **Cook Time:** 20 minutes

> 1 **tablespoon vegetable oil**
> 1 **pound skinless, boneless chicken breasts, cut into strips**
> 1 **can (10¾ ounces) CAMPBELL'S Condensed Golden Mushroom Soup**
> 3 **tablespoons soy sauce**
> 1 **teaspoon garlic powder**
> 1 **bag (16 ounces) frozen vegetable combination, thawed**
> 4 **cups hot Broth Simmered Rice (page 38)**

1. In medium skillet over medium-high heat, heat oil. Add chicken and stir-fry until browned and juices evaporate.

2. Add soup, soy sauce and garlic powder. Heat to a boil. Add vegetables and cook over medium heat until vegetables are tender-crisp, stirring often. Serve over rice.   *Serves 4*

Asian Turkey Stir-Fry: Substitute 2 cups cubed cooked turkey for chicken and oil. Omit step 1. In step 2 in medium skillet over medium heat, heat soup, soy sauce and garlic powder to a boil. Add turkey and vegetables and cook until vegetables are tender-crisp, stirring often.

timesaver tip

To thaw vegetables, microwave on HIGH 4 minutes.

Chicken Quesadillas

(photo on front cover)
Prep Time: 5 minutes   **Cook Time:** 15 minutes

    1 pound skinless, boneless chicken breasts, cubed
    1 can (10¾ ounces) CAMPBELL'S Condensed
       Cheddar Cheese Soup
    ½ cup PACE Thick & Chunky Salsa *or* Picante Sauce
       (medium)
    10 flour tortillas (8-inch)

1. Preheat oven to 425°F.

2. In medium nonstick skillet over medium-high heat, cook chicken
5 minutes or until no longer pink and juices evaporate, stirring
often. Add soup and salsa. Heat through, stirring occasionally.

3. Place tortillas on 2 baking sheets. Top **half** of each tortilla with
about ⅓ cup soup mixture. Spread to within ½ inch of edge.
Moisten edges of tortilla with water. Fold over and seal edges
together.

4. Bake 5 minutes or until hot.   *Serves 4*

Tip: Serve with Fiesta Rice (page 87).

timesaver tip

Substitute 2 cans (5 ounces **each**) SWANSON
Premium Chunk Chicken Breast, drained, for fresh
chicken. In step 2 in medium saucepan mix soup,
salsa and chicken. Over medium heat, heat through,
stirring often. Proceed as in step 3.

Campbell's

15-Minute Chicken & Rice Dinner

Prep/Cook Time: 15 minutes

> 1 **tablespoon vegetable oil**
> 4 **skinless, boneless chicken breast halves (about 1 pound)**
> 1 **can (10¾ ounces) CAMPBELL'S Condensed Cream of Chicken Soup** *or* **98% Fat Free Cream of Chicken Soup**
> 1½ **cups water**
> ¼ **teaspoon paprika**
> ¼ **teaspoon pepper**
> 1½ **cups uncooked Minute® Original Rice**
> 2 **cups fresh** *or* **thawed frozen broccoli flowerets**

1. In medium skillet over medium-high heat, heat oil. Add chicken and cook 8 minutes or until browned. Set chicken aside. Pour off fat.

2. Add soup, water, paprika and pepper. Heat to a boil.

3. Stir in rice and broccoli. Place chicken on rice mixture. Reduce heat to low. Cover and cook 5 minutes or until chicken is no longer pink. *Serves 4*

Chicken & Rice Dinner with Green Beans: Substitute 2 cups fresh *or* thawed frozen cut green beans for broccoli.

tip

For creamier rice, increase water to 1⅔ cups.

15-Minute Chicken & Rice Dinner

Easy Chicken & Pasta

Prep Time: 5 minutes   **Cook Time:** 25 minutes

> 1 **tablespoon vegetable oil**
> 1 **pound skinless, boneless chicken breasts, cut up**
> 1 **can (10¾ ounces) CAMPBELL'S Condensed Cream of Mushroom Soup or 98% Fat Free Cream of Mushroom Soup**
> 2¼ **cups water**
> ½ **teaspoon dried basil leaves, crushed**
> 2 **cups frozen vegetable combination (broccoli, cauliflower, carrots)**
> 2 **cups uncooked corkscrew macaroni**
>   **Grated Parmesan cheese**

1. In medium skillet over medium-high heat, heat oil. Add chicken and cook until browned, stirring often. Set chicken aside.

2. Add soup, water, basil and vegetables. Heat to a boil. Add **uncooked** macaroni. Reduce heat to medium. Cook 10 minutes, stirring often.

3. Return chicken to pan. Cook 5 minutes more or until macaroni is done, stirring often. **Sprinkle with cheese.**   *Serves 4*

Your Choice Chicken & Pasta:

Choose a soup...	Choose a pasta...	Choose a combo...
CAMPBELL'S Condensed Cream of Chicken Soup or 98% Fat Free Cream of Chicken Soup	Uncooked medium tube-shaped macaroni	Broccoli, corn and red peppers combination
CAMPBELL'S Condensed Cheddar Cheese Soup	Uncooked spaghetti, broken in half*	Stir-fry or Oriental vegetables, no sauce added
CAMPBELL'S Condensed Cream of Celery Soup or 98% Fat Free Cream of Celery Soup	Uncooked bow tie pasta	Peas and carrots

Increase water to 2½ cups. 8 ounces uncooked spaghetti = 2 cups.

Easy Chicken & Pasta

for Easy Chicken & Pasta

Grandma

tions / TBL VEGETABLE OIL

ESS, BONELESS CHICKEN BREAST

PBELL'S CREAM OF MUSHROOM

ER

BASIL LEAVES, CRUSHED

VEG. COMBINAT

Quick Chicken Parmigiana

Prep Time: 5 minutes   **Cook Time:** 15 minutes

---

1 package (about 10 ounces) frozen fully cooked
  breaded chicken patties *or* 1 package (about
  14 ounces) refrigerated fully cooked breaded
  chicken cutlets
1 jar (28 ounces) PREGO Traditional Pasta Sauce
2 tablespoons grated Parmesan cheese
½ cup shredded mozzarella cheese (2 ounces)
4 cups hot cooked spaghetti (about 8 ounces
  uncooked)

1. In 2-quart shallow baking dish arrange patties. Top each with
¼ *cup* pasta sauce. Sprinkle with Parmesan cheese and
mozzarella cheese.

2. Bake at 400°F. for 15 minutes or until chicken is hot and cheese
is melted.

3. Heat remaining sauce until hot. Serve sauce with chicken and
spaghetti.   *Serves 4*

Time Saver: In 2-quart shallow microwave-safe baking dish arrange
patties. Microwave on HIGH 4 minutes (3 minutes for refrigerated
cutlets). Top each patty with ¼ *cup* pasta sauce, *1 teaspoon*
Parmesan cheese and *2 tablespoons* mozzarella cheese. Microwave
2 minutes more or until sauce is hot and cheese is melted.

Chicken Nuggets Parmigiana: Substitute 1 package (10 to
13 ounces) frozen *or* refrigerated fully cooked breaded chicken
nuggets for chicken patties. In 2-quart shallow microwave-safe
baking dish arrange nuggets. Microwave on HIGH 3½ minutes
(2½ minutes for refrigerated). Pour pasta sauce evenly over nuggets.
Top with cheeses. Microwave 2 minutes more or until sauce is hot
and cheese is melted.

Top to bottom: *Mushroom Mozzarella Bruschetta (page 69)
and Quick Chicken Parmigiana*

Skillet Herb Roasted Chicken

Prep Time: 10 minutes   **Cook Time:** 20 minutes

> 4 skinless, boneless chicken breast halves (about 1 pound)
> ¼ teaspoon ground sage
> ¼ teaspoon dried thyme leaves, crushed
> Vegetable cooking spray
> 2 cloves garlic, minced
> 1 can (10¾ ounces) CAMPBELL'S HEALTHY REQUEST Condensed Cream of Chicken Soup
> ½ cup water
> 4 cups hot cooked rice, cooked without salt

1. Sprinkle chicken with sage and thyme.

2. Spray medium nonstick skillet with cooking spray and heat over medium heat 1 minute. Add chicken and cook 15 minutes or until chicken is browned and no longer pink. Remove and keep warm.

3. Remove pan from heat. Spray with cooking spray. Add garlic and cook 30 seconds or until lightly browned.

4. Add soup and water. Reduce heat to low and heat through. Serve over chicken with rice.

Serves 4

Nutritional Values per Serving: Calories 457, Total Fat 5g, Saturated Fat 2g, Cholesterol 79mg, Sodium 361mg, Total Carbohydrate 65g, Protein 33g

Tip: Serve with **Herb Broth Simmered Rice:** In medium saucepan over medium-high heat, heat 1 can (16 ounces) CAMPBELL'S HEALTHY REQUEST Ready to Serve Chicken Broth to a boil. Add 1 cup uncooked regular long-grain white rice and ½ teaspoon dried thyme leaves, crushed. Reduced heat to low. Cover and cook 25 minutes or until rice is done and most of liquid is absorbed.

Skillet Herb Roasted Chicken

Country Mustard Chicken

Prep Time: 5 minutes   **Cook Time:** 20 minutes

Vegetable cooking spray
4 skinless, boneless chicken breast halves
1 jar (12 ounces) FRANCO-AMERICAN Slow Roast Chicken Gravy
1 tablespoon country-style Dijon mustard
½ teaspoon garlic powder

1. Spray medium skillet with cooking spray and heat over medium-high heat 1 minute. Add chicken and cook 10 minutes or until browned. Set chicken aside.

2. Add gravy, mustard and garlic powder. Heat to a boil. Return chicken to pan. Reduce heat to low. Cover and cook 5 minutes or until chicken is no longer pink. Serve with noodles if desired. Sprinkle with chopped parsley.   *Serves 4*

QUICK SIDE DISH Broccoli & Noodles Supreme

Prep Time: 5 minutes   **Cook Time:** 20 minutes

3 cups *uncooked* medium egg noodles
2 cups fresh *or* frozen broccoli flowerets
1 can (10¾ ounces) CAMPBELL'S Condensed Cream of Chicken & Broccoli Soup
½ cup sour cream
⅓ cup grated Parmesan cheese
⅛ teaspoon pepper

In large saucepan prepare noodles according to package directions. Add broccoli for last 5 minutes of cooking time. Drain. In same pan mix soup, sour cream, cheese, pepper and noodle mixture. Over medium heat, heat through, stirring occasionally.   *Serves 5*

Left to right: Broccoli & Noodles Supreme and Country Mustard Chicken

Tomato-Basil Chicken

Prep Time: 5 minutes   **Cook Time:** 20 minutes

1 tablespoon vegetable oil
4 skinless, boneless breast halves (about 1 pound)
1 can (10¾ ounces) CAMPBELL'S Condensed Tomato
   Soup
½ cup milk
2 tablespoons grated Parmesan cheese
½ teaspoon dried basil leaves, crushed
¼ teaspoon garlic powder *or* 2 cloves garlic, minced
4 cups hot cooked medium tube-shaped macaroni
   (about 3 cups uncooked)

1. In medium skillet over medium-high heat, heat oil. Add chicken and cook 10 minutes or until browned. Set chicken aside. Pour off fat.

2. Add soup, milk, cheese, basil and garlic powder. Heat to a boil. Return chicken to pan. Reduce heat to low. Cover and cook 5 minutes or until chicken is no longer pink. Serve with macaroni.

Serves 4

tip

Cook pasta as chicken is browning. For extra flavor, simmer pasta in broth (see Simple Seasoned Pasta, page 26).

Top to Bottom: *Honey-Mustard Chicken (page 28)* *and Tomato-Basil Chicken*

Crunchy No-Fry Chicken

Prep Time: 10 minutes   **Cook Time:** 20 minutes

> ¾ **cup finely crushed corn flakes**
> ½ **teaspoon garlic powder**
> ⅛ **teaspoon black pepper**
> ⅛ **teaspoon ground red pepper**
> 4 **skinless, boneless chicken breast halves**
> ¼ **cup SWANSON Chicken Broth**

1. Mix corn flakes, garlic powder, black pepper and red pepper. Dip chicken into broth. Coat with corn flake mixture.

2. Place chicken on baking sheet. Bake at 400°F. for 20 minutes or until chicken is no longer pink.   *Serves 4*

QUICK SIDE DISH Glazed Snow Peas & Carrots

Prep Time: 15 minutes   **Cook Time:** 10 minutes

> 4 **teaspoons cornstarch**
> 1 **can (14½ ounces) SWANSON Vegetable Broth**
> 4 **medium carrots, sliced (about 2 cups)**
> 1 **medium onion, chopped (about ½ cup)**
> ¾ **pound snow peas (about 4 cups)**
> 1 **teaspoon lemon juice**

1. In cup mix cornstarch and *1 cup* broth until smooth. Set aside.

2. In medium skillet over high heat, heat remaining broth to a boil. Add carrots and onion. Reduce heat to medium. Cover and cook 5 minutes or until carrots are tender-crisp. Add snow peas. Cook 2 minutes.

3. Stir cornstarch mixture and add. Cook until mixture boils and thickens, stirring constantly. Stir in lemon juice.   *Serves 8*

Left to right: Crunchy No-Fry Chicken, Glazed Snow Peas & Carrots and Garlic Mashed Potatoes (page 85)

Lemon Broccoli Chicken

Prep Time: 5 minutes   **Cook Time:** 20 minutes

---

1 **lemon**
1 **tablespoon vegetable oil**
4 **skinless, boneless chicken breast halves (about
    1 pound)**
1 **can (10¾ ounces) CAMPBELL'S Condensed Cream
    of Broccoli Soup** *or* **98% Fat Free Cream of
    Broccoli Soup**
¼ **cup milk**
⅛ **teaspoon pepper**

1. Cut 4 thin slices of lemon and set aside. Squeeze 2 teaspoons juice from remaining lemon and set aside.

2. In medium skillet over medium-high heat, heat oil. Add chicken and cook 10 minutes or until browned. Set chicken aside. Pour off fat.

3. Add soup, milk, reserved lemon juice and pepper. Heat to a boil. Return chicken to pan. Top with lemon slices. Reduce heat to low. Cover and cook 5 minutes or until chicken is no longer pink.

Serves 4

tip

Looking for a quick and delicious side dish your family will love? Top your favorite cooked pasta shape with PREGO Pasta Sauce, a perfect accompaniment to chicken, pork or meat loaf!

Lemon Broccoli Chicken

25-Minute Chicken & Noodles

Prep Time: 10 minutes   **Cook Time:** 15 minutes

- **1 can (14½ ounces) SWANSON Chicken Broth (1¾ cups)**
- **½ teaspoon dried basil leaves, crushed**
- **⅛ teaspoon pepper**
- **2 cups frozen vegetable combination (broccoli, cauliflower, carrots)**
- **2 cups *uncooked* medium egg noodles**
- **2 cups cubed cooked chicken**

1. In medium skillet mix broth, basil, pepper and vegetables. Over medium-high heat, heat to a boil. Reduce heat to medium. Cover and cook 5 minutes.

2. Stir in noodles. Cover and cook 5 minutes, stirring often. Add chicken and heat through.   *Serves 4*

tip

For 2 cups cubed cooked chicken: In medium saucepan over medium heat, in 4 cups boiling water, cook 1 pound skinless, boneless chicken breasts *or* thighs, cubed, 5 minutes or until chicken is no longer pink. Chicken should be cooked to a minimum internal temperature of 165°F.

Chicken Mozzarella

Prep Time: 10 minutes   **Cook Time:** 20 minutes

> 4 skinless, boneless chicken breast halves (about
>   1 pound)
> 1 can (10¾ ounces) CAMPBELL'S HEALTHY REQUEST
>   Condensed Tomato Soup
> ½ teaspoon Italian seasoning *or* dried oregano
>   leaves, crushed
> ½ teaspoon garlic powder
> ¼ cup shredded mozzarella cheese (1 ounce)
> 4 cups hot cooked corkscrew macaroni (about 3 cups
>   uncooked), cooked without salt

1. Place chicken in 2-quart shallow baking dish. Mix soup, Italian seasoning and garlic powder. Spoon over chicken and bake at 400°F. for 20 minutes or until chicken is no longer pink.

2. Sprinkle cheese over chicken. Remove chicken. Stir sauce. Serve with macaroni.   *Serves 4*

Nutritional Values per Serving: Calories 559, Total Fat 7g, Saturated Fat 2g, Cholesterol 78mg, Sodium 385mg, Total Carbohydrate 80g, Protein 41g

QUICK SIDE DISH Simple Seasoned Pasta

Prep Time: 5 minutes   **Cook Time:** 15 minutes

> 1 can (14½ ounces) SWANSON Seasoned Chicken
>   Broth with Italian Herbs
> 1½ cups *uncooked* corkscrew macaroni

In medium saucepan over medium-high heat, heat broth to a boil. Stir in macaroni. **Reduce heat to medium.** Simmer gently 10 minutes or until macaroni is done, stirring occasionally.   *Serves 2*

Chicken Mozzarella and Simple Seasoned Pasta

Texts Two-Step Chicken Picante

Prep Time: 5 minutes   **Cook Time:** 20 minutes

4 skinless, boneless chicken breast halves
1½ cups PACE Picante Sauce *or* Thick & Chunky Salsa
3 tablespoons packed light brown sugar
1 tablespoon Dijon-style mustard

1. Place chicken in 2-quart shallow baking dish. Mix picante sauce, sugar and mustard. Pour over chicken.

2. Bake at 400°F. for 20 minutes or until chicken is no longer pink. Serve with hot cooked rice if desired.   *Serves 4*

Honey-Mustard Chicken

(photo on page 19)
Prep Time: 10 minutes   **Cook Time:** 20 minutes

1 tablespoon butter *or* margarine
4 skinless, boneless chicken breast halves
1 can (10¾ ounces) CAMPBELL'S Condensed Cream of Chicken Soup *or* 98% Fat Free Cream of Chicken Soup
¼ cup mayonnaise
2 tablespoons honey
1 tablespoon spicy brown mustard
Chopped toasted pecans *or* walnuts

1. In medium skillet over medium-high heat, heat butter. Add chicken and cook 10 minutes or until browned. Set chicken aside.

2. Add soup, mayonnaise, honey and mustard. Heat to a boil. Return chicken to pan. Reduce heat to low. Cover and cook 5 minutes or until chicken is no longer pink. Sprinkle with pecans. Serve with rice if desired.   *Serves 4*

Top to bottom: *Mexican-Style Mac 'n' Cheese (page 59), Queso Baked Potato (page 84) and Texas Two-Step Chicken Picante*

Chicken Dijon

Prep Time: 5 minutes   **Cook Time:** 20 minutes

Vegetable cooking spray
4 skinless, boneless chicken breast halves (about
  1 pound)
1 can (10¾ ounces) CAMPBELL'S Condensed Cream
  of Celery Soup *or* 98% Fat Free Cream of Celery
  Soup
⅔ cup water
1 tablespoon Dijon-style mustard
⅛ teaspoon pepper
4 cups hot cooked rice

1. Spray medium skillet with cooking spray and heat over medium-high heat 1 minute. Add chicken and cook 10 minutes or until browned. Set chicken aside.

2. Add soup, water, mustard and pepper. Heat to a boil. Return chicken to pan. Reduce heat to low. Cover and cook 5 minutes or until chicken is no longer pink. Serve with rice.   *Serves 4*

tip

The versatile Vegetable Stir-Fry (page 59),
pictured right as a side dish, also works as a main
dish served over rice.

Left to right: *Vegetable Stir-Fry (page 59)
and Chicken Dijon*

Santa Fe Chicken

Prep Time: 10 minutes   **Cook Time:** 20 minutes

1 tablespoon all-purpose flour
1 tablespoon chili powder
4 skinless, boneless chicken breast halves (about
  1 pound)
2 tablespoons vegetable oil
1 can (10¾ ounces) CAMPBELL'S Condensed Tomato
  Soup
¼ cup shredded Cheddar *or* Monterey Jack cheese
  (1 ounce)

1. Mix flour and chili powder. Coat chicken with flour mixture.

2. In medium skillet over medium heat, heat oil. Add chicken and cook 10 minutes or until browned. Set chicken aside. Pour off fat.

3. Add soup. Heat to a boil. Return chicken to pan. Reduce heat to low. Cover and cook 5 minutes or until chicken is no longer pink. Sprinkle with cheese.   *Serves 4*

QUICK SIDE DISH Simple Two-Step Nacho Pasta

Prep Time: 5 minutes   **Cook Time:** 20 minutes

4 cups *uncooked* corkscrew macaroni
1 can (11 ounces) CAMPBELL'S Condensed Fiesta
  Nacho Cheese Soup
½ cup milk

1. In large saucepan prepare macaroni according to package directions. Drain.

2. In same pan mix soup, milk and macaroni. Over medium heat, heat through, stirring often.   *Serves 4*

Left to right: *Simple Two-Step Nacho Pasta
and Santa Fe Chicken*

Crispy Chicken with Asparagus Sauce

Prep Time: 10 minutes   **Cook Time:** 20 minutes

    4 skinless, boneless chicken breast halves *or*
       8 skinless, boneless chicken thighs (about
       1 pound)
    1 egg *or* 2 egg whites, beaten
  ½ cup dry bread crumbs
    2 tablespoons vegetable oil
    1 can (10¾ ounces) CAMPBELL'S Condensed Cream
       of Asparagus Soup
  ⅓ cup milk
  ⅓ cup water
    Grated Parmesan cheese

1. Dip chicken into egg. Coat with bread crumbs.

2. In medium skillet over medium heat, heat oil. Add chicken and cook 15 minutes or until chicken is browned and no longer pink. Remove and keep warm. Pour off fat.

3. Add soup, milk and water. Reduce heat to low and heat through. Serve over chicken. Sprinkle with cheese. Serve with rice if desired.   *Serves 4*

tip

Try this dish over Broth Simmered Rice (page 38), with vegetables steamed in broth.

Top to bottom: *Crispy Chicken with Asparagus Sauce and Quick Lemon-Broccoli Rice (page 87)*

Campbell's

MEAT DISHES IN MINUTES

Shortcut Beef Stew

Prep Time: 5 minutes   **Cook Time:** 25 minutes

- 1 tablespoon vegetable oil
- 1 pound boneless beef sirloin steak, cut into 1-inch cubes
- 1 can (10¾ ounces) CAMPBELL'S Condensed Tomato Soup
- 1 can (10¾ ounces) CAMPBELL'S Condensed Beefy Mushroom Soup
- 1 tablespoon Worcestershire sauce
- 1 bag (24 ounces) frozen vegetables for stew (potatoes, carrots, celery)

1. In Dutch oven over medium-high heat, heat oil. Add beef and cook until browned, stirring often. Set beef aside.

2. Add soups, Worcestershire and vegetables. Heat to a boil. Return beef to pan. Reduce heat to low. Cover and cook 10 minutes or until vegetables are tender, stirring occasionally.

Serves 4

Shortcut Beef Stew

Beef & Broccoli

Prep Time: 10 minutes   **Cook Time:** 20 minutes

---

   1 **pound boneless beef sirloin** *or* **top round steak,**
     ¾ inch thick
   1 **tablespoon vegetable oil**
   1 **can (10¾ ounces) CAMPBELL'S Condensed Tomato**
    › **Soup**
   3 **tablespoons soy sauce**
   1 **tablespoon vinegar**
   1 **teaspoon garlic powder**
  ¼ **teaspoon red pepper flakes (optional)**
   3 **cups fresh** *or* **thawed frozen broccoli flowerets**

1. Slice beef into very thin strips.

2. In medium skillet over medium-high heat, heat oil. Add beef and stir-fry until browned and juices evaporate.

3. Add soup, soy sauce, vinegar, garlic powder and pepper flakes. Heat to a boil. Add broccoli and cook over medium heat until broccoli is tender-crisp, stirring often. Serve with Broth Simmered Rice. *Serves 4*

QUICK
SIDE DISH **Broth Simmered Rice**

Prep/Cook Time: 10 minutes   **Stand Time:** 5 minutes

---

   1 **can (10½ ounces) CAMPBELL'S Condensed Chicken**
     Broth
  ¾ **cup water**
   2 **cups uncooked Minute® Original Rice**

In medium saucepan over medium-high heat, heat broth and water to a boil. Stir in rice. Cover and remove from heat. Let stand 5 minutes. Fluff with fork. *Serves 4*

Left to right: *Beef & Broccoli and Broth Simmered Rice*

Easy Spaghetti & Meatballs

Prep Time: 15 minutes   **Cook Time:** 10 minutes

    1 pound ground beef
    2 tablespoons water
    ⅓ cup seasoned dry bread crumbs
    1 egg, beaten
    1 jar (28 ounces) PREGO Traditional Pasta Sauce *or* Pasta Sauce Flavored with Meat
    4 cups hot cooked spaghetti

1. Mix beef, water, bread crumbs and egg. Shape meat mixture into 12 (2-inch) meatballs. Arrange in 2-quart shallow microwave-safe baking dish.

2. Microwave on HIGH 5 minutes or until meatballs are no longer pink (160°F.). Pour off fat. Pour pasta sauce over meatballs. Cover and microwave 3 minutes more or until sauce is hot. Serve over spaghetti.   *Serves 4*

Zesty Ziti

Prep Time: 10 minutes   **Cook Time:** 20 minutes

    1 pound Italian sausage, cut into ½-inch pieces
    1 large onion, chopped (about 1 cup)
    1 medium green pepper, diced (about 1 cup)
    1 jar (28 ounces) PREGO Three Cheese Pasta Sauce
    4½ cups hot cooked medium tube-shaped macaroni

1. In medium skillet over medium heat, cook sausage, onion and pepper until sausage is no longer pink. Pour off fat.

2. Add pasta sauce. Heat to a boil. Serve over macaroni. Top with grated Parmesan cheese.   *Serves 4*

Top to bottom: Zesty Ziti and Easy Spaghetti & Meatballs

Fiesta Taco Salad

Prep Time: 10 minutes   **Cook Time:** 15 minutes

- **1 pound ground beef**
- **2 tablespoons chili powder**
- **1 can (10¾ ounces) CAMPBELL'S Condensed Tomato Soup**
- **8 cups salad greens torn into bite-size pieces**
- **2 cups tortilla chips**
- **Chopped tomato**
- **Sliced green onions**
- **Shredded Cheddar cheese**
- **Sliced pitted ripe olives**

1. In medium skillet over medium-high heat, cook beef and chili powder until beef is browned, stirring to separate meat. Pour off fat.

2. Add soup. Reduce heat to low and heat through.

3. Arrange salad greens and chips on platter. Spoon meat mixture over salad greens. Top with tomato, onions, cheese and olives.

Serves 4

timesaver tip

Save time by using packaged pre-shredded Cheddar cheese and checking the salad bar at your supermarket for pre-cut greens, toppers and trimmings.

Fiesta Taco Salad

Two-Bean Chili

Prep Time: 10 minutes   **Cook Time:** 15 minutes

- 1 pound ground beef
- 1 large green pepper, chopped (about 1 cup)
- 1 large onion, chopped (about 1 cup)
- 2 tablespoons chili powder
- ¼ teaspoon black pepper
- 3 cups CAMPBELL'S Tomato Juice
- 1 can (about 15 ounces) kidney beans, rinsed and drained
- 1 can (about 15 ounces) great Northern *or* white kidney (cannellini) beans, rinsed and drained
  Sour cream
  Sliced green onions
  Shredded Cheddar cheese
  Chopped tomato

1. In medium skillet over medium-high heat, cook beef, green pepper, onion, chili powder and black pepper until beef is browned, stirring to separate meat. Pour off fat.

2. Add tomato juice and beans and heat through. Top with sour cream, green onions, cheese and tomato.   *Serves 6*

For a cool refresher, mix ¾ cup CAMPBELL'S Tomato Juice with ¼ cup ginger ale and 1 tablespoon lemon juice. Serve over ice and garnish with lemon slice.

Top to bottom: *Hearty Vegetarian Chili (page 58)*
and Two-Bean Chili

Spicy Salsa Mac & Beef

Prep Time: 5 minutes   **Cook Time:** 25 minutes

 1 **pound ground beef**
 1 **can (10½ ounces) CAMPBELL'S Condensed Beef
    Broth**
1⅓ **cups water**
 2 **cups** *uncooked* **medium shell** *or* **elbow macaroni**
 1 **can (10¾ ounces) CAMPBELL'S Condensed
    Cheddar Cheese Soup**
 1 **cup PACE Thick & Chunky Salsa**

1. In medium skillet over medium-high heat, cook beef until browned, stirring to separate meat. Pour off fat.

2. Add broth and water. Heat to a boil. Stir in macaroni. Reduce heat to medium. Cook 10 minutes or until macaroni is done, stirring often.

3. Stir in soup and salsa and heat through.   *Serves 4*

tip

Pair this dynamic kid-pleasing dish with a glass of V8 SPLASH. The light taste of tropical fruit juices makes a great go-with and delivers 100% of Vitamins A and C.

Spicy Salsa Mac & Beef

Quick Pepper Steak

Prep Time: 10 minutes   **Cook Time:** 20 minutes

- 1 **pound boneless beef sirloin *or* top round steak,**
  ¾ inch thick
- 2 **tablespoons vegetable oil**
- 2 **medium green *or* red peppers, cut into 2-inch-long**
  strips (about 3 cups)
- 1 **medium onion, cut into wedges**
- ½ **teaspoon garlic powder**
- 1 **can (10¼ ounces) FRANCO-AMERICAN Beef Gravy**
- 1 **tablespoon Worcestershire sauce**
- 4 **cups hot cooked rice**

1. Slice beef into thin strips.

2. In medium skillet over medium-high heat, heat *half* the oil. Add beef in 2 batches and stir-fry until browned. Set beef aside.

3. Reduce heat to medium. Add remaining oil. Add peppers, onion and garlic powder and stir-fry until tender-crisp. Pour off fat.

4. Add gravy and Worcestershire. Heat to a boil. Return beef to pan. Reduce heat to low and heat through. Serve over rice.

Serves 4

tip

Instead of choosing either green or red peppers,
try both together to vary the flavor and create
a colorful dish!

Quick Pepper Steak

Picante Beef & Beans

Prep Time: 10 minutes   **Cook Time:** 20 minutes

- **2 tablespoons cornstarch**
- **2 tablespoons water**
- **1 tablespoon vegetable oil**
- **1 pound boneless beef sirloin steak, cut into 1-inch cubes**
- **1 tablespoon chili powder**
- **¾ cup PACE Picante Sauce *or* Thick & Chunky Salsa**
- **1 can (about 16 ounces) black beans, undrained**
- **1 can (about 15 ounces) pinto beans, undrained**
- **1 can (about 14½ ounces) stewed tomatoes**

1. In cup mix cornstarch and water until smooth. Set aside.

2. In Dutch oven over medium-high heat, heat oil. Add beef and chili powder and cook until beef is browned, stirring often.

3. Add picante sauce, beans and tomatoes. Heat to a boil. Reduce heat to low. Cover and cook 5 minutes or until beef is done.

4. Stir cornstarch mixture and add. Cook until mixture boils and thickens, stirring constantly.   *Serves 6*

tip

PACE Picante Sauce and Thick & Chunky Salsa are
available in mild, medium and hot varieties.
Try the one your family likes best.

Picante Beef & Beans

Southwest Skillet

Prep/Cook Time: 20 minutes   **Stand Time:** 5 minutes

- ¾ **pound ground beef**
- 1 **tablespoon chili powder**
- 1 **can (10¾ ounces) CAMPBELL'S Condensed Beefy Mushroom Soup**
- ¼ **cup water**
- 1 **can (about 15 ounces) kidney beans, rinsed and drained**
- 1 **can (14½ ounces) whole peeled tomatoes, cut up**
- ¾ **cup uncooked Minute® Original Rice**
- ½ **cup shredded Cheddar cheese (2 ounces)**
- **Crumbled tortilla chips**

1. In medium skillet over medium-high heat, cook beef and chili powder until browned, stirring to separate meat. Pour off fat.

2. Add soup, water, beans and tomatoes. Heat to a boil. Reduce heat to low. Cover and cook 10 minutes.

3. Stir in rice. Remove from heat. Cover and let stand 5 minutes. Top with cheese and chips.   *Serves 4*

tip

Store ground meat in the coldest part of the refrigerator (40°F.) for up to 2 days. Be sure to cook ground meat thoroughly until browned, to a minimum 155°F.

Top to bottom: Ham & Pasta Skillet (page 54) and Southwest Skillet

Mushroom Garlic Pork Chops

Prep Time: 5 minutes **Cook Time:** 20 minutes

> 1 tablespoon vegetable oil
> 4 pork chops, ½ inch thick (about 1 pound)
> 1 can (10¾ ounces) CAMPBELL'S Condensed Cream
>   of Mushroom with Roasted Garlic Soup
> ¼ cup water

1. In medium skillet over medium-high heat, heat oil. Add chops and cook 10 minutes or until browned. Set chops aside. Pour off fat.

2. Add soup and water. Heat to a boil. Return chops to pan. Reduce heat to low. Cover and cook 5 minutes or until chops are no longer pink.

Serves 4

Ham & Pasta Skillet

(photo on page 53)
Prep Time: 10 minutes **Cook Time:** 15 minutes

> 1 can (10¾ ounces) CAMPBELL'S Condensed Broccoli
>   Cheese Soup
> 1 cup milk
> 1 tablespoon spicy brown mustard
> 2 cups broccoli flowerets *or* 1 package (10 ounces)
>   frozen broccoli cuts (2 cups)
> 1½ cups cooked ham strips
> 3 cups cooked medium shell macaroni (about 2 cups
>   uncooked)

In medium skillet mix soup, milk, mustard and broccoli. Over medium heat, heat to a boil. Reduce heat to low. Cook 5 minutes or until broccoli is tender. Add ham and macaroni and heat through.

Serves 4

Mushroom Garlic Pork Chop

Campbell's

EASY FISH & MEATLESS

Garlic Shrimp & Pasta

Prep Time: 15 minutes   **Cook Time:** 10 minutes

- 1 **can (14½ ounces) SWANSON Chicken Broth (1¾ cups)**
- 2 **cloves garlic, minced**
- 3 **tablespoons chopped fresh parsley** *or* **1 tablespoon dried parsley flakes**
- 2 **tablespoons cornstarch**
- 2 **tablespoons lemon juice**
- ⅛ **teaspoon ground red pepper**
- 1 **pound medium shrimp, shelled and deveined**
- 4 **cups hot cooked thin spaghetti (about 8 ounces uncooked)**

1. In medium saucepan mix broth, garlic, parsley, cornstarch, lemon juice and pepper. Over medium-high heat, heat to a boil. Cook until mixture thickens, stirring constantly.

2. Add shrimp. Cook 5 minutes more or until shrimp turn pink, stirring often. Toss with spaghetti.   *Serves 4*

Top to bottom: *Quick 'n' Easy Salmon (page 58), Vegetable Rice Pilaf (page 86) and Garlic Shrimp & Pasta*

Quick 'n' Easy Salmon

(photo on page 57)
Prep Time: 5 minutes   **Cook Time:** 15 minutes

- 1 can (14½ ounces) SWANSON Chicken Broth (1¾ cups)
- ¼ cup Chablis *or* other dry white wine
- ¼ teaspoon dried dill weed, crushed
- 4 thin lemon slices
- 4 salmon steaks, 1 inch thick (about 1½ pounds)

1. In medium skillet mix broth, wine, dill and lemon. Over medium-high heat, heat to a boil.

2. Place fish in broth mixture. Reduce heat to low. Cover and cook 10 minutes or until fish flakes easily when tested with a fork. Discard poaching liquid. *Serves 4*

Hearty Vegetarian Chili

(photo on page 45)
Prep Time: 10 minutes   **Cook Time:** 20 minutes

- 2 tablespoons vegetable oil
- 1 large onion, chopped (about 1 cup)
- 1 small green pepper, chopped (about ½ cup)
- ¼ teaspoon garlic powder *or* 2 cloves garlic, minced
- 1 tablespoon chili powder
- ½ teaspoon ground cumin
- 2½ cups V8 100% Vegetable Juice
- 1 can (16 ounces) black beans, rinsed and drained
- 1 can (15 ounces) pinto beans, rinsed and drained

1. In large saucepan over medium heat, heat oil. Add onion, pepper, garlic powder, chili powder and cumin and cook until tender.

2. Add vegetable juice. Heat to a boil. Reduce heat to low. Cook 5 minutes. Add beans and heat through. *Serves 4*

Vegetable Stir-Fry

(photo on page 31)
Prep Time: 15 minutes **Cook Time:** 10 minutes

  1 **can (14½ ounces) SWANSON Vegetable Broth**
  2 **tablespoons cornstarch**
  1 **tablespoon soy sauce**
  ¼ **teaspoon ground ginger**
  1 **tablespoon vegetable oil**
  5 **cups cut-up vegetables***
  ⅛ **teaspoon garlic powder *or* 1 clove garlic, minced**

1. In bowl mix broth, cornstarch, soy sauce and ginger until smooth. Set aside.

2. In medium skillet over medium-high heat, heat oil. Add vegetables and garlic powder and stir-fry until tender-crisp.

3. Stir cornstarch mixture and add. Cook until mixture boils and thickens, stirring constantly.

Serves 4 as a main dish or 8 as a side dish

Use a combination of broccoli flowerets, sliced mushrooms, sliced carrots, sliced celery, red or green pepper strips and sliced green onions.

Mexican-Style Mac 'n' Cheese

(photo on page 29)
Prep Time: 5 minutes **Cook Time:** 10 minutes

  2 **cups *uncooked* elbow macaroni**
  1 **jar (15 ounces) PACE Picante con Queso Dip**

1. In large saucepan prepare macaroni according to package directions. Drain.

2. In same pan mix dip and macaroni. Over low heat, heat through, stirring occasionally. *Serves 4*

Cajun Fish

Prep Time: 10 minutes **Cook Time:** 15 minutes

> 1 tablespoon vegetable oil
> 1 small green pepper, diced (about ⅔ cup)
> ½ teaspoon dried oregano leaves, crushed
> 1 can (10¾ ounces) CAMPBELL'S Condensed Tomato
> Soup
> ⅓ cup water
> ⅛ teaspoon garlic powder
> ⅛ teaspoon black pepper
> ⅛ teaspoon ground red pepper
> 1 pound firm white fish fillets (cod, haddock or halibut)

1. In medium skillet over medium heat, heat oil. Add green pepper and oregano and cook until tender-crisp, stirring often. Add soup, water, garlic powder, black pepper and red pepper. Heat to a boil.

2. Place fish in soup mixture. Reduce heat to low. Cover and cook 5 minutes or until fish flakes easily when tested with a fork. Serve with rice if desired. *Serves 4*

QUICK SIDE DISH **Slim & Savory Vegetables**

Prep Time: 15 minutes **Cook Time:** 10 minutes

> 1 can (14½ ounces) SWANSON Chicken Broth
> (1¾ cups)
> 4 cups cut-up vegetables*

In medium saucepan mix broth and vegetables. Over medium-high heat, heat to a boil. Reduce heat to low. Cover and cook 5 minutes or until vegetables are tender-crisp. Drain. *Serves 6*

Use a combination of broccoli flowerets, cauliflower flowerets, sliced carrot and sliced celery.

Left to right: *Cajun Fish and Slim & Savory Vegetables*

Primavera Fish Fillets

Prep Time: 10 minutes   **Cook Time:** 20 minutes

- **1** large carrot, cut into matchstick-thin strips (about 1 cup)
- **2** stalks celery, cut into matchstick-thin strips (about 1 cup)
- **1** small onion, diced (about ¼ cup)
- **¼** cup water
- **2** tablespoons Chablis *or* other dry white wine
- **½** teaspoon dried thyme leaves, crushed
  Generous dash pepper
- **1** can (10¾ ounces) CAMPBELL'S HEALTHY REQUEST Condensed Cream of Mushroom Soup
- **1** pound firm white fish fillets (cod, haddock or halibut)

1. In medium skillet mix carrot, celery, onion, water, wine, thyme and pepper. Over medium-high heat, heat to a boil. Reduce heat to low. Cover and cook 5 minutes or until vegetables are tender-crisp.

2. Stir in soup. Over medium heat, heat to a boil.

3. Place fish in soup mixture. Reduce heat to low. Cover and cook 5 minutes or until fish flakes easily when tested with a fork.

Serves 4

Nutritional Values per Serving: Calories 152, Total Fat 2g, Saturated Fat 1g, Cholesterol 45mg, Sodium 414mg, Total Carbohydrate 11g, Protein 19g

> In this recipe, CAMPBELL'S HEALTHY REQUEST creates a lower fat alternative to a traditional Newburg-style sauce made with butter and cream.

Primavera Fish Fillet

Campbell's

Seafood & Mushroom Shells

Bake Time: 30 minutes*   **Prep/Cook Time:** 20 minutes

- 1 package (10 ounces) PEPPERIDGE FARM Frozen Puff Pastry Shells
- 4 tablespoons unsalted butter
- 2½ cups thinly sliced mushrooms (about 8 ounces)
- 1 can (10¾ ounces) CAMPBELL'S Condensed Cream of Mushroom Soup *or* 98% Fat Free Cream of Mushroom Soup
- ½ cup dry white wine *or* vermouth
- 1 tablespoon lemon juice
- 1 pound firm white fish (cod, haddock or halibut), cut into 1-inch pieces
- ½ cup grated Parmesan cheese

1. Bake pastry shells according to package directions.

2. In medium skillet over medium heat, heat butter. Add mushrooms and cook until tender.

3. Add soup, wine, lemon juice and fish. Cook 5 minutes or until fish flakes easily when tested with a fork.

4. Serve in pastry shells. Sprinkle with cheese.   *Serves 4*

*Bake pastry shells while preparing fish mixture.

Top to bottom: *Seafood & Mushroom Shells and Creamy Vegetables in Pastry Shells (page 89)*

Campbell's
SPEEDY SNACKS & MINI-MEALS

Chicken Noodle Soup Express

Prep Time: 10 minutes   **Cook Time:** 15 minutes

> 2 cans (14½ ounces *each*) SWANSON Chicken Broth
> (3½ cups)
> Generous dash pepper
> 1 medium carrot, sliced (about ½ cup)
> 1 stalk celery, sliced (about ½ cup)
> ½ cup *uncooked* medium egg noodles
> 1 can (5 ounces) SWANSON Premium Chunk Chicken
> Breast *or* Chunk Chicken, drained

In medium saucepan mix broth, pepper, carrot and celery. Over medium-high heat, heat to a boil. Stir in noodles. Reduce heat to medium. Cook 10 minutes, stirring often. Add chicken and heat through.

Serves 4

Top to bottom: Easy Vegetable Soup (page 68) and Chicken Noodle Soup Express

Easy Vegetable Soup

(photo on page 67)
Prep Time: 5 minutes   **Cook Time:** 25 minutes

**2 cans (14½ ounces *each*) SWANSON Chicken Broth
(3½ cups)**
3 cups CAMPBELL'S Tomato Juice
**1 teaspoon dried oregano leaves *or* Italian
seasoning, crushed**
½ teaspoon garlic powder *or* 4 cloves garlic, minced
¼ teaspoon pepper
**1 bag (16 ounces) frozen vegetable combination
(broccoli, cauliflower, carrots)**
**1 can (about 15 ounces) kidney beans *or* 1 can (about
16 ounces) white kidney (cannellini) beans, rinsed
and drained**

In large saucepan mix broth, tomato juice, oregano, garlic powder,
pepper and vegetables. Over medium-high heat, heat to a boil.
Cover and cook 10 minutes or until vegetables are tender. Add
beans and heat through.   *Serves 8*

tip

For a change of taste, substitute 1 bag (16 ounces)
frozen Italian vegetable combination.

Mushroom Mozzarella Bruschetta

(photo on page 13)
Prep Time: 15 minutes   **Cook Time:** 5 minutes

1 loaf (about 1 pound) Italian bread (16 inches long),
   cut in half lengthwise
1 can (10¾ ounces) CAMPBELL'S Condensed Cream
   of Mushroom Soup *or* 98% Fat Free Cream of
   Mushroom Soup
¼ teaspoon garlic powder
¼ teaspoon dried Italian seasoning, crushed
1 cup shredded mozzarella cheese (4 ounces)
1 tablespoon grated Parmesan cheese
1 small red pepper, chopped (about ½ cup)
2 green onions, chopped (about ¼ cup)

1. Bake bread on baking sheet at 400°F. for 5 minutes or until lightly toasted.

2. Mix soup, garlic powder and Italian seasoning. Stir in mozzarella cheese, Parmesan cheese, pepper and onions.

3. Spread soup mixture on bread. Bake 5 minutes or until cheese is melted. Cut each bread half into 4 pieces.   *Serves 8*

timesaver tip

For convenience, use packaged pre-shredded
mozzarella cheese. Half an 8-ounce package will
provide the 1 cup needed for this recipe.

Chicken Broccoli Pockets

Prep Time: 15 minutes   **Cook Time:** 10 minutes

- 1 can (10¾ ounces) CAMPBELL'S HEALTHY REQUEST Condensed Cream of Chicken Soup
- ¼ cup water
- 1 tablespoon lemon juice
- ¼ teaspoon garlic powder
- ⅛ teaspoon pepper
- 1 cup cooked broccoli flowerets
- 1 medium carrot, shredded (about ½ cup)
- 2 cups cubed cooked chicken
- 3 pita breads (6-inch), cut in half, forming 2 pockets

1. In medium saucepan mix soup, water, lemon juice, garlic powder, pepper, broccoli, carrot and chicken. Over medium heat, heat through.

2. Spoon ½ cup chicken mixture into each pita half.

Makes 6 sandwiches

Nutritional Values per Serving: Calories 202, Total Fat 4g, Saturated Fat 1g, Cholesterol 39mg, Sodium 404mg, Total Carbohydrate 24g, Protein 16g

Chicken Broccoli Potato Topper: Omit pita breads. Serve ¾ cup chicken mixture over each of 4 hot baked potatoes, split (about 2 pounds). *Serves 4*

> In this recipe, CAMPBELL'S HEALTHY REQUEST provides a healthier, delicious alternative to a mayonnaise-based pocket sandwich filling.

Top to bottom: Creamy Risotto (page 88) and Chicken Broccoli Pocket

Souperburger Sandwiches

Prep Time: 5 minutes   **Cook Time:** 10 minutes

- 1 **pound ground beef**
- 1 **medium onion, chopped (about ½ cup)**
- 1 **can (10¾ ounces) CAMPBELL'S Condensed Cheddar Cheese Soup**
- 1 **tablespoon prepared mustard**
- ⅛ **teaspoon pepper**
- 6 **hamburger rolls, split and toasted**

1. In medium skillet over medium-high heat, cook beef and onion until beef is browned, stirring to separate meat. Pour off fat.

2. Add soup, mustard and pepper. Reduce heat to low and heat through. Divide meat mixture among rolls.

Makes 6 sandwiches

Sausage & Pepper Sandwiches

Prep Time: 10 minutes   **Cook Time:** 10 minutes

- 1 **pound bulk pork sausage**
- 1 **small green pepper, chopped (about ½ cup)**
- 1 **can (11⅛ ounces) CAMPBELL'S Condensed Italian Tomato Soup**
- 4 **long sandwich rolls, split**

1. In medium skillet over medium-high heat, cook sausage and pepper until sausage is browned, stirring to separate meat. Pour off fat.

2. Add soup. Reduce heat to low and heat through. Divide meat mixture among rolls.

Makes 4 sandwiches

Top to bottom: Souperburger Sandwich, Sausage & Pepper Sandwich and Shortcut Sloppy Joe (page 74)

5-Minute Burrito Wraps

Prep/Cook Time: 5 minutes

> 1 can (11¼ ounces) CAMPBELL'S Condensed Fiesta
>   Chili Beef Soup
> 6 flour tortillas (8-inch)
>   Shredded Cheddar cheese

1. Spoon 2 tablespoons soup down center of each tortilla. Top with cheese. Fold tortilla around filling.

2. Place seam-side down on microwave-safe plate and microwave on HIGH 2 minutes or until hot.   *Makes 6 burritos*

Shortcut Sloppy Joes

(photo on page 73)
Prep Time: 5 minutes   **Cook Time:** 10 minutes

> 1 pound ground beef
> 1 can (11⅛ ounces) CAMPBELL'S Condensed Italian
>   Tomato Soup
> ¼ cup water
> 2 teaspoons Worcestershire sauce
> ⅛ teaspoon pepper
> 6 hamburger rolls, split and toasted

1. In medium skillet over medium-high heat, cook beef until browned, stirring to separate meat. Pour off fat.

2. Add soup, water, Worcestershire and pepper. Reduce heat to low and heat through. Divide meat mixture among rolls.

                                          Makes 6 sandwiches

5-Minute Burrito Wraps

Quick Beef 'n' Beans Tacos

Prep Time: 15 minutes   **Cook Time:** 10 minutes

- 1 **pound ground beef**
- 1 **small onion, chopped (about ¼ cup)**
- 1 **can (11¼ ounces) CAMPBELL'S Condensed Fiesta Chili Beef Soup**
- ¼ **cup water**
- 10 **taco shells**
  Shredded Cheddar cheese, shredded lettuce, diced tomato and sour cream

1. In medium skillet over medium-high heat, cook beef and onion until beef is browned, stirring to separate meat. Pour off fat.

2. Add soup and water. Reduce heat to low. Cover and cook 5 minutes.

3. Divide meat mixture among taco shells. Top with cheese, lettuce, tomato and sour cream.   *Makes 10 tacos*

Deluxe Nachos

Prep Time: 10 minutes   **Cook Time:** 5 minutes

- 1 **can (about 16 ounces) black beans, drained**
- 1 **bag (about 9 ounces) tortilla chips**
- 1 **jar (15 ounces) PACE Picante con Queso Dip**
- 1 **medium tomato, chopped (about 1 cup)**
- ¼ **cup sliced pitted ripe olives**
- 2 **green onions, sliced (about ¼ cup)**

Spread beans over tortilla chips. Heat dip according to package directions. Spoon over tortilla chips. Top with tomato, olives and onions.   *Serves 6*

Top to bottom: Deluxe Nachos and Quick Beef 'n' Beans Tacos

Cheesy Broccoli Potato Topper

Prep Time: 5 minutes   **Cook Time:** 5 minutes

> 1 can (10¾ ounces) CAMPBELL'S Condensed
>   Cheddar Cheese Soup
> 4 large hot baked potatoes, split
> 1 cup cooked broccoli flowerets

1. Stir soup in can until soup is smooth.

2. Place hot baked potatoes on microwave-safe plate. Carefully fluff up potatoes with fork.

3. Top each potato with broccoli. Spoon soup over potatoes. Microwave on HIGH 4 minutes or until hot.   *Serves 4*

Baked Potatoes Olé

Prep Time: 5 minutes   **Cook Time:** 15 minutes

> 1 pound ground beef
> 1 tablespoon chili powder
> 1 cup PACE Picante Sauce *or* Thick & Chunky Salsa
> 4 hot baked potatoes, split
>   Shredded Cheddar cheese

1. In medium skillet over medium-high heat, cook beef and chili powder until beef is browned, stirring to separate meat. Pour off fat.

2. Add picante sauce. Reduce heat to low and heat through. Serve over potatoes. Top with cheese.   *Serves 4*

Clockwise from top: Cheesy Picante Potatoes (page 85), Baked Potato Olé and Cheesy Broccoli Potato Topper

Campbell's
QUICK SIDE DISHES

One-Dish Pasta & Vegetables

Prep Time: 15 minutes   **Cook Time:** 15 minutes

- 1½ cups *uncooked* corkscrew macaroni
- 2 medium carrots, sliced (about 1 cup)
- 1 cup broccoli flowerets
- 1 can (10¾ ounces) CAMPBELL'S Condensed Cheddar Cheese Soup
- ½ cup milk
- 1 tablespoon prepared mustard

1. In large saucepan prepare macaroni according to package directions. Add carrots and broccoli for last 5 minutes of cooking time. Drain.

2. In same pan mix soup, milk, mustard and macaroni mixture. Over medium heat, heat through, stirring often.   *Serves 5*

Quick Onion Fries

Prep Time: 5 minutes   **Cook Time:** about 20 minutes

> 1 pouch CAMPBELL'S Dry Onion Soup and Recipe Mix
> 3 tablespoons vegetable oil
> 1 package (about 22 ounces) frozen French-fried potatoes

1. In large bowl mix soup mix and oil. Add potatoes. Toss to coat.

2. Bake according to package directions, stirring occasionally.

Serves 6

Saucy Asparagus

Prep Time: 10 minutes   **Cook Time:** 15 minutes

> 1 can (10¾ ounces) CAMPBELL'S Condensed Cream of Asparagus Soup
> 2 tablespoons milk
> 1½ pounds asparagus, trimmed, cut into 1-inch pieces (about 3 cups) *or* 2 packages (10 ounces *each*) frozen asparagus cuts

1. In medium saucepan mix soup and milk. Over medium heat, heat to a boil, stirring occasionally.

2. Add asparagus. Reduce heat to low. Cover and cook 10 minutes or until asparagus is tender, stirring occasionally.   *Serves 6*

Top to bottom: *Quick Onion Fries and Saucy Asparagus*

Queso Baked Potatoes

(photo on page 29)
Prep Time: 10 minutes   **Cook Time:** 3 minutes

4 hot baked potatoes, split
1 cup PACE Picante con Queso Dip

1. Place hot baked potatoes on microwave-safe plate. Carefully fluff up potatoes with fork.

2. Spoon dip over potatoes. Microwave on HIGH 3 minutes or until hot.

Serves 4

To heat one potato: Top with ¼ cup dip. Microwave on HIGH 1 minute or until hot. Increase time to 2 minutes if using dip from the refrigerator.

Broccoli Queso Baked Potatoes: In step 2 top each potato with ¼ cup cooked broccoli cuts. Spoon dip over potatoes. Microwave on HIGH 3 minutes or until hot.

Vegetable Queso Baked Potatoes: After microwaving potatoes with dip, top each potato with chopped tomato and sliced green onion.

To bake potatoes, pierce potatoes with fork. Bake at 400°F. for 1 hour *or* microwave on HIGH 10½ to 12½ minutes or until fork-tender.

Garlic Mashed Potatoes

(photo on page 21)
Prep Time: 10 minutes   **Cook Time:** 15 minutes

> **2 cans (14½ ounces *each*) SWANSON Seasoned
> Chicken Broth with Roasted Garlic**
> **5 large potatoes, cut into 1-inch pieces**

1. In medium saucepan place broth and potatoes. Over high heat, heat to a boil. Reduce heat to medium. Cover and cook 10 minutes or until potatoes are tender. Drain, reserving broth.

2. Mash potatoes with *1¼ cups* reserved broth. If needed, add additional broth until potatoes are desired consistency.

Serves about 6

Skinny Mashed Potatoes: Substitute 2 cans (14½ ounces *each*) SWANSON Chicken Broth for Chicken Broth with Roasted Garlic.

Cheesy Picante Potatoes

(photo on page 79)
Prep Time: 10 minutes   **Cook Time:** 10 minutes

> **1 can (10¾ ounces) CAMPBELL'S Condensed
> Cheddar Cheese Soup**
> **½ cup PACE Picante Sauce *or* Thick & Chunky Salsa**
> **1 teaspoon garlic powder**
> **4 cups cubed cooked potatoes (about 4 medium)
> Paprika**
> **2 tablespoons chopped fresh cilantro**

In medium skillet mix soup, picante sauce and garlic powder. Add potatoes. Over medium heat, heat through, stirring often. Sprinkle with paprika and cilantro. Serve with additional picante sauce.

Serves 6 to 8

Vegetable-Rice Pilaf

(photo on page 57)
Prep Time: 5 minutes   **Cook Time:** 20 minutes

Vegetable cooking spray
¼ cup chopped green *or* red pepper
2 cloves garlic, minced
½ teaspoon dried basil leaves, crushed
⅛ teaspoon black pepper
1 cup *uncooked* regular long-grain white rice
1 can (16 ounces) CAMPBELL'S HEALTHY REQUEST
   Ready to Serve Chicken Broth
¾ cup frozen mixed vegetables

1. Spray medium skillet with cooking spray and heat over medium heat 1 minute. Add green pepper, garlic, basil, black pepper and rice. Cook until rice is browned and green pepper is tender-crisp, stirring constantly.

2. Stir in broth. Heat to a boil. Reduce heat to low. Cover and cook 10 minutes.

3. Stir in vegetables. Cover and cook 10 minutes more or until rice is done and most of liquid is absorbed.   *Serves 4*

Nutritional Values per Serving: Calories 204, Total Fat 1g, Saturated Fat 0g, Cholesterol 0mg, Sodium 241mg, Total Carbohydrate 43g, Protein 6g

Try this delicious side dish as a healthier alternative to high-sodium packaged rice dishes.

Fiesta Rice

(photo on front cover)

Prep Time: 5 minutes   **Cook/Stand Time:** 10 minutes

> 1 can (10½ ounces) CAMPBELL'S Condensed Chicken Broth
> ½ cup water
> ½ cup PACE Thick & Chunky Salsa
> 2 cups uncooked Minute® Original Rice

1. In medium saucepan mix broth, water and salsa. Over medium-high heat, heat to a boil.

2. Stir in rice. Cover and remove from heat. Let stand 5 minutes. Fluff with fork.   *Serves 4*

Quick Lemon-Broccoli Rice

(photo on page 35)

Prep Time: 10 minutes   **Cook Time:** 15 minutes

> 1 can (10½ ounces) CAMPBELL'S Condensed Chicken Broth
> 1 cup small broccoli flowerets
> 1 small carrot, shredded (about ⅓ cup)
> 1¼ cups uncooked Minute® Original Rice
> 2 teaspoons lemon juice
> Generous dash pepper

1. In medium saucepan over high heat, heat broth to a boil. Add broccoli and carrot. Reduce heat to low. Cover and cook 5 minutes or until vegetables are tender.

2. Stir in rice, lemon juice and pepper. Cover and remove from heat. Let stand 5 minutes. Fluff with fork.   *Serves 4*

Creamy Risotto

(photo on page 71)

Prep Time: 5 minutes   **Cook/Stand Time:** 15 minutes

1 can (10¾ ounces) CAMPBELL'S HEALTHY REQUEST Condensed Cream of Mushroom Soup
1½ cups CAMPBELL'S HEALTHY REQUEST Ready to Serve Chicken Broth
1½ cups uncooked Minute® Original Rice
1 tablespoon grated Parmesan cheese
Pepper

1. In medium saucepan mix soup and broth. Over medium-high heat, heat to a boil.

2. Stir in rice and cheese. Cover and remove from heat. Let stand 10 minutes. Fluff with fork. Serve with freshly ground pepper and additional cheese if desired.

Serves 4

Nutritional Values per Serving: Calories 191, Total Fat 2g, Saturated Fat 1g, Cholesterol 7mg, Sodium 480mg, Total Carbohydrate 36g, Protein 5g

Tomato-Basil Risotto: In step 2, add 1 tablespoon chopped fresh basil *or* ¼ teaspoon dried basil leaves, crushed, and 1 small tomato, diced (about ½ cup) *or* ½ cup drained cut-up canned tomatoes with rice.

Use HEALTHY REQUEST to lighten up your favorite dishes such as this international specialty—easily and deliciously.

Creamy Vegetables in Pastry Shells

(photo on page 65)
Bake Time: 30 minutes*   **Prep/Cook Time:** 15 minutes

- 1 package (10 ounces) PEPPERIDGE FARM Frozen Puff Pastry Shells
- 1 can (10¾ ounces) CAMPBELL'S Condensed Cream of Mushroom Soup *or* 98% Fat Free Cream of Mushroom Soup
- ⅓ cup milk *or* water
- 1 bag (16 ounces) frozen vegetable combination (broccoli, cauliflower, carrots), cooked and drained

1. Prepare pastry shells according to package directions.

2. In medium saucepan mix soup and milk. Over medium heat, heat through, stirring often. Divide vegetables among pastry shells. Spoon sauce over vegetables and pastry shells.

Serves 6

Bake pastry shells while preparing sauce mixture.

 **tip**

Substitute 2 cups broccoli flowerets, 1 cup cauliflowerets and 2 medium carrots, sliced (about 2 cups), cooked and drained, for the frozen vegetable combination.

Recipe Index

Product Index

Notes

Notes

Notes

Campbell's

Metric Conversion Chart

VOLUME MEASUREMENTS (dry)

⅛ teaspoon = 0.5 mL
¼ teaspoon = 1 mL
½ teaspoon = 2 mL
¾ teaspoon = 4 mL
1 teaspoon = 5 mL
1 tablespoon = 15 mL
2 tablespoons = 30 mL
¼ cup = 60 mL
⅓ cup = 75 mL
½ cup = 125 mL
⅔ cup = 150 mL
¾ cup = 175 mL
1 cup = 250 mL
2 cups = 1 pint = 500 mL
3 cups = 750 mL
4 cups = 1 quart = 1 L

VOLUME MEASUREMENTS (fluid)

1 fluid ounce (2 tablespoons) = 30 mL
4 fluid ounces (½ cup) = 125 mL
8 fluid ounces (1 cup) = 250 mL
12 fluid ounces (1½ cups) = 375 mL
16 fluid ounces (2 cups) = 500 mL

WEIGHTS (mass)

½ ounce = 15 g
1 ounce = 30 g
3 ounces = 90 g
4 ounces = 120 g
8 ounces = 225 g
10 ounces = 285 g
12 ounces = 360 g
16 ounces = 1 pound = 450 g

DIMENSIONS

1/16 inch = 2 mm
⅛ inch = 3 mm
¼ inch = 6 mm
½ inch = 1.5 cm
¾ inch = 2 cm
1 inch = 2.5 cm

OVEN TEMPERATURES

250°F = 120°C
275°F = 140°C
300°F = 150°C
325°F = 160°C
350°F = 180°C
375°F = 190°C
400°F = 200°C
425°F = 220°C
450°F = 230°C

BAKING PAN SIZES

Utensil	Size in Inches/Quarts	Metric Volume	Size in Centimeters
Baking or	8×8×2	2 L	20×20×5
Cake Pan	9×9×2	2.5 L	23×23×5
(square or	12×8×2	3 L	30×20×5
rectangular)	13×9×2	3.5 L	33×23×5
Loaf Pan	8×4×3	1.5 L	20×10×7
	9×5×3	2 L	23×13×7
Round Layer	8×1½	1.2 L	20×4
Cake Pan	9×1½	1.5 L	23×4
Pie Plate	8×1¼	750 mL	20×3
	9×1¼	1 L	23×3
Baking Dish	1 quart	1 L	—
or Casserole	1½ quart	1.5 L	—
	2 quart	2 L	—